JAVA PROGRAMMING MADE EASY

Unlock Your Coding Potential from Scratch

Ryan Campbell

Table of Contents

Introduction to Java Programming

Welcome to "Java Programming Made Easy: Unlock Your Coding Potential from Scratch." If you've ever been curious about coding and want to dive into the world of Java, then you've come to the right place!

In this book, we'll embark on an exciting journey together, starting from square one and guiding you through the wonderful world of Java programming. Don't worry if you're a complete beginner – we've got your back!

Our goal is to make learning Java a breeze, breaking down complex concepts into bite-sized pieces that are easy to digest. Whether you're a student, a professional looking to enhance your skills, or simply someone with a passion for programming, this book will set you on the path to success.

We'll start by helping you set up your Java development environment, ensuring you have the right tools at your fingertips. From there, we'll dive into the basics, covering variables, data types, and the building blocks of Java programming. With each chapter, you'll gain a deeper understanding and unlock your coding potential.

But it doesn't stop there! We'll explore exciting topics like object-oriented programming, GUI programming with JavaFX, handling databases, and even multithreading. You'll discover how to unleash the true power of Java and develop robust, efficient, and elegant programs.

Throughout the book, we'll provide plenty of examples, exercises, and real-world scenarios to reinforce your learning. And if you ever find yourself stuck or facing coding challenges, fret not! We'll equip you with troubleshooting tips and guide you through common pitfalls, so you can overcome any obstacles with confidence.

So, are you ready to embark on this Java adventure? Get ready to unlock your coding potential and become a master of Java programming. Let's jump right in and start creating amazing things with code!

Happy coding!

Chapter 1: Setting Up Your Java Development Environment

Welcome to Chapter 1 of "Java Programming Made Easy: Unlock Your Coding Potential from Scratch!" In this section, we'll assist you in establishing your Java programming workspace. A proper setup is crucial for a smooth and productive coding experience.

1.1 Why a Proper Development Environment Matters

Before we dive into the setup process, let's take a moment to understand why a proper development environment is essential for your Java programming journey.

Step 1: Streamlined Workflow

A well-configured development environment provides a streamlined workflow, allowing you to write, test, and debug your code efficiently. It provides the necessary tools and features to enhance your productivity and make coding a breeze.

Step 2: Access to Libraries and Frameworks

A proper development environment ensures that you have easy access to libraries, frameworks, and other resources that can significantly simplify your Java development process. It enables you to leverage existing code and solutions, saving you time and effort.

Step 3: Compatibility and Stability

With a properly set up development environment, you ensure compatibility and stability with the Java platform. It allows you to work with the latest versions of Java, ensuring that your code is up to date and follows best practices.

1.2 Installing the Java Development Kit (JDK)

The Java Development Kit (JDK) is an essential component for Java development. It provides the tools and libraries necessary for compiling, running, and debugging Java programs. Let's walk through the installation process.

Step 1: Visit the Oracle JDK Website

To download the JDK, visit the official Oracle JDK website at https://www.oracle.com/java/technologies/javase-jdk11-downloads.html.

Step 2: Accept the License Agreement

On the Oracle JDK website, you'll find a list of available JDK versions. Choose the version appropriate for your operating system and click on the corresponding download link. You will be asked to agree to the terms of the license. Read through the agreement and click "Accept" to proceed with the download.

Step 3: Run the Installer

After the download finishes, execute the installer and adhere to the directions provided on the screen. The installer will guide you through the installation process, including selecting the installation directory and configuring any additional settings.

Step 4: Verify the Installation

After the installation is complete, it's essential to verify that the JDK is installed correctly. Open a command prompt or terminal window and type the following command:

shellCopy code

java -version

If the JDK is installed properly, you should see the Java version information displayed in the terminal.

1.3 Choosing an Integrated Development Environment (IDE)

An Integrated Development Environment (IDE) is a software solution that offers an all-inclusive suite of tools and functionalities for authoring, scrutinizing, and debugging code.

While you can write Java code using a simple text editor, an IDE can greatly enhance your coding experience. Let's explore a few popular IDE options.

Step 1: Eclipse

Eclipse is a commonly utilized open-source IDE designed for crafting Java applications. It offers a rich set of features, including code completion, debugging tools, and a user-friendly interface. To install Eclipse, follow these steps:

1. Visit the Eclipse website at https://www.eclipse.org/ and navigate to the "Downloads" section.

2. Choose the appropriate Eclipse package for Java development based on your operating system.

3. Download the package and run the installer.

Step 2: IntelliJ IDEA

IntelliJ IDEA is a popular commercial IDE developed by JetBrains. It provides advanced coding assistance, intelligent code completion, and powerful debugging capabilities. To install IntelliJ IDEA, follow these steps:

1. Visit the IntelliJ IDEA website at https://www.jetbrains.com/idea/ and navigate to the "Download" section.

2. Choose the appropriate version for your operating system (Community Edition for free or Ultimate Edition for a paid version).

3. Download the installer and run it.

1.4 Configuring Your IDE

Once you've chosen and installed an IDE, it's essential to configure it properly to suit your preferences and optimize your coding experience. Let's explore some common configuration steps.

Step 1: Selecting the JDK

In your IDE settings, ensure that you have selected the correct JDK installation. This ensures that your IDE uses the JDK you installed earlier for compiling and running your Java code.

Step 2: Setting Up Code Formatting

Configuring code formatting rules ensures consistent and readable code. Set up indentation, line wrapping, and other formatting options according to your preferred coding style.

Step 3: Installing Useful Plugins

IDEs often support various plugins that enhance functionality. Explore the available plugins and install those that align with your development needs. Common plugins include Git integration, code analysis tools, and additional language support.

1.5 Creating Your First Java Project

Now that your development environment is all set up, it's time to create your first Java project. Let's walk through the process step by step.

Step 1: Open Your IDE

Launch your IDE, whether it's Eclipse or IntelliJ IDEA, and create a new Java project.

Step 2: Define the Project Name and Location

Specify a name for your project and choose a location on your computer where the project files will be stored. This will create a directory structure for your project.

Step 3: Configure the Project Build Path

Ensure that your project's build path is correctly configured to include the JDK and any necessary libraries. This allows your project to compile and run successfully.

Step 4: Create a Java Class

Create a new Java class within your project. This is where you'll write your Java code. Give the class a meaningful name and start coding!

1.6 Ready for the Java Journey

Congratulations! By installing the JDK, selecting an IDE, and configuring it to suit your needs, you're now well-equipped to start your Java programming journey.

But remember, this is just the beginning. There's so much more to explore and learn in the vast world of Java programming. In the next chapter, we'll dive into the basics of Java syntax and explore how to write your first Java program. Get ready to unleash your coding potential!

Chapter 2: Understanding Variables and Data Types

In this chapter, we'll delve into the fascinating world of variables and data types in Java. Understanding how to work with variables and data types is essential for manipulating and storing different kinds of information in your programs. So, let's get started and explore the fundamentals!

2.1 Introduction to Variables

Variables are containers that hold values in your program. They allow you to store and manipulate data, making your programs dynamic and adaptable. Before we dive into the different types of variables, let's take a moment to understand their significance.

javaCopy code

int age;

javaCopy code

age = 25;

Step 3: Using the Variable

Once a variable is declared and assigned a value, you can use it in your code. For example, you can display the value of the **age** variable using the **System.out.println()** method:

javaCopy code

System.out.println("Age: " + age);

2.2 Primitive Data Types

Java provides several primitive data types that represent basic values, such as numbers and characters. Let's explore the most commonly used primitive data types and their characteristics.

Step 1: Integer Data Types

Integers represent whole numbers without decimal places. In Java, you can choose from several integer data types based on the range of values you need:

- **byte**: Represents a small integer ranging from -128 to 127.

- **short**: Represents a short integer ranging from -32,768 to 32,767.

- **int**: Represents a standard integer ranging from -2,147,483,648 to 2,147,483,647.

- **long**: Represents a large integer ranging from -9,223,372,036,854,775,808 to 9,223,372,036,854,775,807.

Step 2: Floating-Point Data Types

Floating-point numbers represent numbers with decimal places. Java offers two floating-point data types:

- **float**: Represents single-precision floating-point numbers with 32 bits of precision.

- **double**: Represents double-precision floating-point numbers with 64 bits of precision.

Step 3: Character Data Type

The **char** data type represents a single character. It can hold any Unicode character, such as letters, digits, symbols, or even special characters. To assign a character to a **char** variable, enclose it in single quotes (").

2.3 Reference Data Types

In addition to primitive data types, Java also provides reference data types, also known as objects. These data types allow you to work with more complex and customized data structures. Let's explore a few commonly used reference data types.

Step 1: Strings

The **String** class represents a sequence of characters. It allows you to store and manipulate text. To declare a **String** variable, use the **String** class name followed by the variable name. For example:

javaCopy code

String name = "John";

Step 3: Custom Classes

In Java, you can create your own custom classes to represent objects with specific attributes and behaviors. Custom classes allow you to model real-world entities or create specialized data structures to suit your program's needs.

2.4 Type Casting

It's particularly useful when you need to perform operations or assignments between different data types. Let's explore the two types of type casting: implicit casting and explicit casting.

Step 1: Implicit Casting

Implicit casting, also known as widening conversion, happens automatically when you assign a value of a smaller data type to a larger data type. For example, assigning an

int value to a **long** variable is an implicit cast because **long** can accommodate the larger range of **int**.

Step 2: Explicit Casting

Explicit casting, also known as narrowing conversion, requires you to specify the target data type in parentheses before the value. Explicit casting is necessary when you want to assign a larger data type to a smaller data type, potentially resulting in a loss of precision.

2.5 Choosing the Right Data Type

Choosing the appropriate data type is crucial for efficient memory usage and program execution. Let's discuss some guidelines to help you choose the right data type for your variables.

Step 1: Consider Data Range and Precision

Choose a data type that can adequately represent the range of values you need. If you require decimal precision, opt for floating-point data types. For whole numbers, use appropriate integer types.

Step 2: Account for Memory Usage

Consider the memory requirements of your program. Using larger data types when smaller ones suffice can waste memory. Optimize memory usage by selecting the smallest data type that can hold your required values.

Step 3: Ensure Compatibility with Operations

Some operations may have specific data type requirements. Ensure that the data types you choose are compatible with the operations you intend to perform. For example, if you need to perform mathematical calculations, floating-point data types might be necessary.

2.6 Ready to Harness the Power of Variables and Data Types

Congratulations! You've gained a solid understanding of variables and data types in Java. By mastering these concepts, you have the foundation to create dynamic and versatile programs. But remember, this is just the tip of the iceberg in your Java programming journey.

In the next chapter, we'll explore control flow statements, such as conditionals and loops, which allow your programs to make decisions and repeat actions.

Chapter3: Control Flow: Conditionals and Loops

Conditionals, also known as decision-making statements, allow your program to execute different blocks of code based on specified conditions. This gives you the power to control the flow of your program's execution. Let's dive into the most commonly used conditional statements in Java.

Step 1: if Statement

For example, let's say you want to check if a person is eligible to vote. You can use an **if** statement to determine if their age is 18 or above:

javaCopy code

```
int age = 20; if (age >= 18) { System.out.println("You are eligible to vote!"); }
```

For example, let's say you want to check if a number is positive or negative. You can use an **if-else** statement to display the appropriate message:

javaCopy code

```java
int number = -5; if (number > 0) { System.out.println("The number is positive."); } else { System.out.println("The number is negative."); }
```

Step 3: if-else if-else Statement

The **if-else if-else** statement allows you to handle multiple conditions and execute different blocks of code based on those conditions. The syntax is as follows:

For example, let's say you want to assign a letter grade based on a student's score. You can use an **if-else if-else** statement to determine the appropriate grade:

javaCopy code

```java
int score = 75; if (score >= 90) { System.out.println("Grade: A"); } else if (score >= 80) { System.out.println("Grade: B"); } else if (score >= 70) { System.out.println("Grade: C"); } else if (score >= 60) { System.out.println("Grade: D"); } else { System.out.println("Grade: F"); }
```

3.2 Introduction to Loops

Loops allow you to repeat a block of code multiple times, making it easier to perform repetitive tasks and iterate over data structures. Let's explore the different types of loops in Java.

Step 1: for Loop

The **for** loop is used when you know the exact number of iterations you want to perform

You can use a **for** loop to achieve this:

javaCopy code

```
for (int i = 1; i <= 5; i++) { System.out.println(i); }
```

Step 2: while Loop

The **while** loop is used when you want to repeat a block of code as long as a condition is true. The syntax of a **while** loop is as follows:

javaCopy code

```
while (condition) { // Code to be executed as long as the condition is true }
```

For example, let's say you want to print the numbers from 1 to 5 using a **while** loop:

javaCopy code

```
int i = 1; while (i <= 5) { System.out.println(i); i++; }
```

Step 3: do-while Loop

The **do-while** loop is similar to the **while** loop, but it guarantees that the code block is executed at least once, even if the condition is initially false. The syntax of a **do-while** loop is as follows:

javaCopy code

do { // Code to be executed } while (condition);

For example, let's say you want to ask the user for a positive number. You can use a **do-while** loop to repeatedly prompt the user until they enter a positive number:

javaCopy code

int number; do { System.out.println("Enter a positive number: "); number = scanner.nextInt(); } while (number <= 0);

3.3 Breaking and Skipping Loop Iterations

Sometimes, you may need to prematurely exit a loop or skip certain iterations based on specific conditions. Java provides keywords that allow you to achieve these behaviors.

Step 1: break Statement

The **break** statement allows you to exit a loop prematurely, even if the loop condition is still true. It is often used when a certain condition is met, and you want to stop the loop. For example:

javaCopy code

```
for (int i = 1; i <= 10; i++) { if (i == 5) { break; } System
.out.println(i); }
```

vbnetCopy code

In this example, the `break` statement is used to exit the `for` loop when `i` is equal to 5. As a result, only the numbers 1, 2, 3, and 4 will be printed. #### Step 2: continue Statement The `continue` statement allows you to skip the rest of the current iteration and move to the next iteration of the loop. It is often used when you want to skip certain iterations based on a condition. For example: ```java for (int i = 1; i <= 10; i++) { if (i % 2 == 0) { continue; } System.out.println(i); }

In this example, the **continue** statement is used to skip even numbers. When **i** is divisible by 2, the remaining code within the loop is skipped, and the loop moves on to the next iteration.

3.4 Nested Loops

In Java, you can have loops within loops, known as nested loops. This allows you to perform complex iterations and work with multi-dimensional data structures. Let's explore an example of a nested loop.

Step 1: Nested for Loops

Nested **for** loops are commonly used when working with multi-dimensional arrays or performing iterations over two or more variables. For example, let's say you want to print a pattern of stars in the shape of a right triangle:

javaCopy code

```
for (int i = 1; i <= 5; i++) { for (int j = 1; j <= i; j++) {
System.out.print("*"); } System.out.println(); }
```

In this example, the outer loop controls the number of rows, while the inner loop controls the number of stars in each row. As a result, the program will print the following pattern:

markdownCopy code

```
* ** *** **** *****
```

3.5 Ready to Take Control of Your Code

Congratulations! You've gained a solid understanding of control flow in Java. By mastering conditionals and loops, you have the power to make decisions and perform repetitive tasks in your programs.

But remember, this is just the beginning of your coding journey. In the next chapter, we'll explore arrays and ArrayLists, which will enable you to work with collections of data more efficiently. Get ready to level up your coding skills and unlock even more possibilities!

Chapter 4: Arrays and ArrayLists: Working with Collections

Welcome to Chapter 4 of "Java Programming Made Easy: Unlock Your Coding Potential from Scratch!" In this chapter, we'll delve into the powerful world of collections in Java. Collections allow you to store and manipulate groups of related data, making your programs more versatile and efficient. Specifically, we'll explore arrays and ArrayLists, two essential data structures for working with collections. So, let's dive in and discover how to harness the power of collections!

4.1 Introduction to Arrays

Arrays are one of the fundamental data structures in Java. They allow you to store multiple values of the same data type in a single variable. Arrays provide a convenient way to organize and access related data efficiently. Let's explore arrays and their usage in Java.

Step 1: Declaring and Initializing an Array

To work with an array, you first need to declare and initialize it. Here's how you can declare and initialize an array of integers called **numbers** with five elements:

javaCopy code

```java
int[] numbers = new int[5];
```

In this example, we declare an array of integers with the name **numbers** and allocate memory for five elements. By default, the elements in the array will be initialized to their default values (0 for integers).

Step 2: Accessing Array Elements

To access individual elements in an array, you use the index value. The index represents the position of an element in the array, starting from 0. For example, to access the first element in the **numbers** array, you would use the following syntax:

javaCopy code

```java
int firstNumber = numbers[0];
```

In this example, we assign the value of the first element in the **numbers** array to the variable **firstNumber**.

Step 3: Modifying Array Elements

You can also modify the values of array elements using their index. For instance, if you want to change the value of the third element in the **numbers** array to 10, you would write:

javaCopy code

numbers[2] = 10;

In this example, we assign the value 10 to the third element in the **numbers** array.

4.2 Working with ArrayLists

While arrays provide a fixed-size data structure, ArrayLists offer a dynamic alternative that can grow or shrink as needed. ArrayLists are part of the Java Collections Framework and provide additional functionality for managing collections. Let's explore ArrayLists and their usage in Java.

Step 1: Importing the ArrayList Class

Before working with ArrayLists, you need to import the **java.util.ArrayList** class.

javaCopy code

import java.util.ArrayList;

Step 2: Declaring and Initializing an ArrayList

To declare an ArrayList, specify the data type it will hold within angle brackets (<>). For example, to declare an ArrayList of strings called **names**, you would write:

javaCopy code

ArrayList<String> names = new ArrayList<>();

In this example, we declare an ArrayList of strings and initialize it as an empty ArrayList.

Step 3: Adding and Removing Elements

ArrayLists provide methods to add and remove elements dynamically. To add an element to an ArrayList, you can use the **add()** method:

javaCopy code

names.add("Alice");

In this example, we add the string "Alice" to the **names** ArrayList.

To remove an element from an ArrayList, you can use the **remove()** method by specifying either the index or the element itself:

javaCopy code

names.remove(0); // Removes the element at index 0

In this example, we remove the element at index 0 from the **names** ArrayList.

4.3 Common Operations on Collections

Now that we understand the basics of arrays and ArrayLists, let's explore some common operations you can perform on collections.

1. Iterating over Elements

You can iterate over the elements of an array or ArrayList using a loop, such as a **for** loop. This allows you to perform operations on each element or access specific elements based on conditions. Here's an example of iterating over an ArrayList of integers:

javaCopy code

```
for (int i = 0; i < numbers.size(); i++) { int number = numbers.get(i); // Perform operations on 'number' }
```

In this example, we iterate over the elements of the **numbers** ArrayList and assign each element to the **number** variable.

2. Finding the Size of a Collection

To determine the size of an array or ArrayList, you can use the **length** property for arrays and the **size()** method for ArrayLists. Here's an example:

javaCopy code

```
int arraySize = numbers.length; int arrayListSize = names.size();
```

In this example, we store the size of the **numbers** array in the **arraySize** variable and the size of the **names** ArrayList in the **arrayListSize** variable.

3. Sorting Elements

You can sort the elements of an array using the **Arrays.sort()** method. For ArrayLists, you can use the **Collections.sort()** method.

javaCopy code

```
Arrays.sort(numbers);
```

In this example, we sort the elements in the **numbers** array in ascending order.

4. Searching for Elements

To search for an element in an array or ArrayList, you can use a loop to iterate over the collection and compare each element with the target value. Here's an example of searching for a specific name in an ArrayList of strings:

javaCopy code

boolean found = false; for (String name : names) { if (name.equals("Alice")) { found = true; break; } }

In this example, we iterate over the **names** ArrayList and check if any element matches the target name.

4.4 Enhance Your Programs with Collections

Congratulations! You've gained a solid understanding of arrays and ArrayLists in Java. By mastering these collections, you can efficiently store and manipulate groups of related data in your programs. But remember, this is just the beginning.

In the next chapter, we'll explore control flow statements and methods that allow you to manipulate collections in more advanced ways.

Chapter 5: Object-Oriented Programming Principles

Welcome to Chapter 5 of "Java Programming Made Easy: Unlock Your Coding Potential from Scratch!" In this chapter, we'll explore the foundational principles of Object-Oriented Programming (OOP). Object-Oriented Programming is a powerful paradigm that allows you to organize and structure your code in a modular and reusable way. By understanding these principles, you'll be able to create robust and maintainable Java applications.

5.1 Introduction to Object-Oriented Programming (OOP)

Object-Oriented Programming represents a programming approach that is centered on the notion of 'objects'. An object denotes a real-world item or idea, encompassing its specific data (referred to as attributes) and actions (known as methods). OOP promotes the use of classes and objects to model and solve complex problems. Let's explore the core principles of OOP.

1. Encapsulation

Encapsulation is the practice of bundling data and methods that operate on that data within a single unit called a class.

It allows you to hide the internal implementation details and expose only the necessary interfaces to interact with the object. By encapsulating data, you ensure data integrity and provide a clear interface for other code to interact with.

2. Abstraction

Abstraction represents the technique of streamlining intricate systems by highlighting crucial characteristics while concealing non-essential specifics. In OOP, abstraction is achieved through abstract classes and interfaces. Abstract classes define common characteristics and behaviors shared by a group of related classes, while interfaces define a contract that classes must adhere to. By using abstraction, you can create modular and flexible code that is easier to understand and maintain.

3. Inheritance

Inheritance is a mechanism that allows you to define a new class based on an existing class. The new class, called a subclass or derived class, inherits the attributes and behaviors of the existing class, called the superclass or base class. Inheritance promotes code reuse and enables you to create specialized classes that extend the functionality of their parent classes. It helps in organizing and categorizing related classes in a hierarchical manner.

4. Polymorphism

Polymorphism grants the ability to handle objects from diverse classes as if they belong to a shared parent class. It enables you to use a single interface to represent different implementations. Polymorphism is accomplished via two techniques: method overriding and method overloading.

Method overriding allows a subclass to provide its own implementation of a method defined in the superclass, while method overloading allows multiple methods with the same name but different parameters to exist in the same class.

5.2 Creating Classes and Objects

In Java, classes are the building blocks of object-oriented programming. A class is a blueprint that defines the attributes and behaviors that objects of the class will have. Let's explore how to create classes and objects in Java.

1. Declaring a Class

To declare a class, you specify the class keyword, followed by the class name. Here's an example of a class named **Person**:

javaCopy code

public class Person { // Class body }

In this example, we declare a class named **Person**.

2. Defining Class Members

Within a class, you can define member variables (attributes) and member methods (behaviors). Member variables hold the data associated with an object, while member methods define the operations that the object can perform. Here's an example of a class with member variables and methods:

javaCopy code

```java
public class Person { // Member variables private String name; private int age; // Member methods public void setName(String newName) { name = newName; } public String getName() { return name; } public void celebrateBirthday() { age++; } }
```

In this example, the **Person** class has member variables **name** and **age**, as well as member methods **setName()**, **getName()**, and **celebrateBirthday()**.

3. Creating Objects

Once you have defined a class, you can create objects (instances) of that class using the **new** keyword.

5.3 Applying OOP Principles in Practice

Now that you understand the core principles of Object-Oriented Programming and how to create classes and objects, let's explore how to apply these principles in practice.

1. Identify Objects and Their Behaviors

When approaching a problem, start by identifying the objects involved and the behaviors they exhibit. These objects will become your classes, and their behaviors will become the member methods of those classes. For example, in a banking system, you might have objects like **Account**, **Customer**, and **Transaction**.

2. Define Class Relationships

Determine the relationships between classes. This includes identifying inheritance relationships (is-a relationship), where one class inherits from another, and composition relationships (has-a relationship), where one class contains another as a part. Use inheritance and composition to model the relationships between objects accurately.

3. Encapsulate Data and Hide Implementation Details

Encapsulate the data and methods within a class, making sure to hide unnecessary implementation details. Provide public interfaces (methods) that other code can use to interact with the object, while keeping the internal workings of the object hidden.

4. Use Abstraction to Simplify Complexity

Abstract complex systems into simpler and more manageable components. Use abstract classes and interfaces to define common behaviors and create modular code that can be easily extended and reused.

5. Leverage Inheritance and Polymorphism

Use inheritance to create specialized classes that inherit properties and behaviors from parent classes. Take advantage of polymorphism to treat objects of different classes as objects of a common superclass, enabling code reusability and flexibility.

5.4 Embrace the Power of OOP

Congratulations! You've gained a solid understanding of the object-oriented programming principles in Java. By applying these principles, you can create well-structured, modular, and reusable code. But remember, mastering object-oriented programming is an ongoing process that requires practice and experience.

Chapter 6: Classes and Objects: Building the Foundation

Welcome to Chapter 6 of *Java Programming Made Easy: Unlock Your Coding Potential from Scratch*. As computer engineers, it is essential to grasp the principles of object-oriented programming (OOP) and understand how to create classes and objects effectively. By mastering these concepts, you will be able to build a strong foundation for your Java applications. So, let's dive in and explore the world of classes and objects!

6.1 The Essence of Object-Oriented Programming

Object-oriented programming (OOP) is a paradigm that allows us to structure our programs around objects, which represent real-world entities or concepts. In OOP, a class serves as a blueprint for creating objects, defining their attributes (data) and behaviors (methods). By encapsulating data and related functionality within objects, we can model complex systems and solve problems in a modular and maintainable manner.

As computer engineers, we strive to design software systems that are efficient, reusable, and scalable. Object-oriented programming provides us with a powerful framework to achieve these goals. By leveraging classes and objects, we can create software components that can be easily understood, modified, and extended. Let's dive deeper into the key concepts of classes and objects.

6.2 Creating Classes: Blueprints for Objects

A class functions as a schema or prototype that outlines the organization and actions of objects. It serves as a blueprint from which we can create multiple instances, known as objects. When designing a class, we need to carefully consider its attributes and methods, ensuring they accurately represent the characteristics and behaviors of the real-world entity or concept we are modeling.

6.2.1 Class Structure and Syntax

In Java, a class is declared using the **class** keyword, followed by the class name. Let's take a look at an example of a class representing a car:

javaCopy code

public class Car { // Class body }

In this example, we declare a class named **Car**. The class body, enclosed within curly braces, will contain the member variables (attributes) and member methods (behaviors) of the car objects.

6.2.2 Member Variables: Defining Object Attributes

Member variables, also known as instance variables or fields, represent the attributes or state of an object. They hold the data associated with each object of the class. When defining member variables, consider the properties that are essential to the object being modeled. For our **Car** class, we might include variables such as **make, model, year**, and **mileage**:

javaCopy code

public class Car { private String make; private String model; private int year; private double mileage; // Other member variables }

In this example, we declare member variables **make, model, year**, and **mileage** of appropriate data types (**String, int**, and **double**).

6.2.3 Member Methods: Enabling Object Behaviors

Member methods define the behaviors or actions that objects of a class can perform. They encapsulate the functionality related to the objects and allow them to interact with the outside world. Member methods can manipulate the object's data, perform calculations, provide information, or trigger specific actions. Let's add some member methods to our **Car** class:

javaCopy code

```
public class Car { private String make; private String
model; private int year; private double mileage; public void
startEngine() { // Code to start the car's engine } public
void accelerate() { // Code to accelerate the car } public
void brake() { // Code to apply the car's brakes } // Other
member methods }
```

In this example, we define member methods **startEngine()**, **accelerate()**, and **brake()** to represent the behaviors of starting the engine, accelerating the car, and applying the brakes, respectively.

6.3 Creating Objects: Instances of Classes

Once we have defined a class, we can create multiple instances of that class, known as objects. Each object has its own set of member variables, storing unique data, and can invoke member methods to perform specific actions. Creating objects allows us to bring our classes to life and utilize their defined behaviors.

6.3.1 Instantiating Objects

In Java, we instantiate an object using the **new** keyword, followed by the class name and parentheses. Let's create some car objects based on our **Car** class:

javaCopy code

```
public class Car { // Member variables and methods public static void main(String[] args) { Car car1 = new Car(); Car car2 = new Car(); // Other objects } }
```

In this example, we create two car objects **car1** and **car2** using the **Car** class. Each object has its own memory space to hold the values of member variables.

6.3.2 Accessing Member Variables and Invoking Methods

Once we have created objects, we can access their member variables and invoke their member methods using the dot notation (**.**). Let's demonstrate how we can interact with the car objects we created:

javaCopy code

```
public class Car { private String make; private String model; private int year; private double mileage; // Other member variables and methods public static void main(String[] args) { Car car1 = new Car(); car1.make = "Toyota"; car1.model = "Camry"; car1.year = 2021;
```

```
car1.mileage = 5000.0; System.out.println("Car 1: " +
car1.make + " " + car1.model + ", Year: "

car1.year + ", Mileage: " + car1.mileage);

Car car2 = new Car(); car2.make = "Honda"; car2.model =
"Civic"; car2.year = 2020; car2.mileage = 3000.0;
System.out.println("Car 2: " + car2.make + " " +
car2.model + ", Year:

// Accessing member variables System.out.println("Car 1
make: " + car1.make); System.out.println("Car 2 model: " +
car2.model);

// Invoking member methods car1.startEngine();
car2.accelerate(60); } }
```

In the example above, we created two car objects: car1 and car2. We assigned values to their member variables using the dot notation, where we specify the object name followed by a dot and the variable name. For example, car1.make = "Toyota" assigns the value "Toyota" to the make variable of car1.

To access the member variables of the car objects, we can use the dot notation as well. In the code snippet, we printed the make and model of car1 and car2 using the println() method. We concatenated the values with strings to create meaningful output.

Similarly, we can invoke member methods using the dot notation. In the example, we called the startEngine() method on car1, which presumably starts the engine of the car. We also called the accelerate() method on car2, passing 60 as an argument, which might accelerate the car to a speed of 60 units.

By accessing member variables and invoking member methods, we can interact with objects and perform operations on them. This allows us to manipulate the state and behavior of objects in our Java programs.

Chapter 7: Inheritance and Polymorphism: Extending Functionality

In the previous chapters, we've taken a deep dive into understanding fundamental programming constructs and object-oriented programming (OOP) concepts, particularly encapsulation and abstraction. Now, let's turn our attention to two more pillars of OOP: inheritance and polymorphism. These are key tools for building modular, reusable, and scalable code structures. I'll be your guide as we delve into this fascinating realm.

7.1 Understanding Inheritance

This is an incredibly powerful tool for reducing redundancy and increasing code reusability. In real-world terms, you could think of inheritance as a child inheriting traits from their parent.

Let's say we have a base class named 'Shape' with properties like color and methods like calculateArea(). If we want to create a new class 'Circle', instead of defining all properties and methods from scratch, we can simply have the Circle class inherit from the Shape class. In programming parlance, Shape would be the 'superclass' or 'parent class', and Circle would be the 'subclass' or 'child class'.

7.2 Syntax of Inheritance

In Java, for instance, inheritance is declared using the 'extends' keyword, like so: **class Circle extends Shape { ... }**. In Python, we use a similar approach with a slightly different syntax: **class Circle(Shape): ....** These syntaxes clearly denote that Circle is a subclass of Shape, therefore acquiring its properties and methods.

7.3 Polymorphism

Moving on to polymorphism - a Greek word meaning "many shapes".This can be achieved either through method overloading or method overriding, both leading to the capability of one thing, one name, exhibiting different behaviors.

7.4 Method Overloading and Overriding

Method overloading refers to defining multiple methods with the same name but with different parameters. It's akin to a multi-talented person who can do different tasks depending upon the resources at hand.

In contrast, method overriding involves redefining a method in a subclass that has already been defined in its superclass. This is analogous to a child forming their own version of a story originally told by their parent.

7.5 Inheritance and Polymorphism in Practice

Let's bring these concepts to life with an example. Suppose we're designing a system for a zoo. We have a base class, 'Animal', which contains properties like 'name', 'age', and a method, 'sound()'. This class could be inherited by other classes like 'Lion', 'Elephant', and 'Bird'. Each subclass could have its own unique methods, like 'roar()' for Lion or 'fly()' for Bird, extending the functionality of the base class.

Polymorphism comes into play when we want to iterate over a list of different animals and invoke the 'sound()' method, without needing to know the specific animal type. This is possible because each animal class overrides the 'sound()' method from the Animal superclass in its own way.

7.6 The Power of Inheritance and Polymorphism

The power of inheritance lies in its ability to promote code reusability and maintainability. By grouping common properties and behaviors into a superclass, we create a single source of truth that can be expanded upon by subclasses. This not only reduces redundancy but also makes code easier to manage and maintain.

Polymorphism, on the other hand, bestows flexibility. It allows us to write more generalized code that can work with objects of different classes, as long as they share a common superclass. This means we can write code that is adaptable to new requirements and changes, making our applications more scalable and robust.

7.7 Conclusion

As we conclude this chapter, let's recapture what we learned. Inheritance and polymorphism, when used judiciously, can significantly enhance the modularity and flexibility of our code. As we develop more complex applications, these OOP principles will become increasingly critical in handling the intricacies of our software architecture.

Remember, like any powerful tool, the art lies not just in understanding how to use these concepts, but in knowing when to apply them. Always think carefully about your program's needs before deciding which tools to employ. Keep practicing and exploring different scenarios, and you'll soon become adept at leveraging the power of inheritance and polymorphism.

Chapter 8: Exception Handling: Dealing with Errors

In previous chapters, we explored how to structure and build our code to enhance reusability and scalability. Now, let's focus on a fundamental aspect of robust programming: exception handling. Writing code that performs as expected is essential, but anticipating and handling situations when things go awry is equally crucial.

8.1 Understanding Exceptions

An exception signifies an event happening amidst the running of a program, causing a disruption to the usual sequence of commands. This could be due to logical errors, runtime errors, or unforeseen conditions like a network outage or a file not found. Exception handling provides a structured, consistent method to deal with these errors and ensure that our program can continue to function or fail gracefully.

8.2 Try-Catch Blocks

The most common way to handle exceptions is using try-catch blocks. The segment of code that holds the possibility of triggering an exception is positioned within the 'try' block. If an exception occurs, the flow of control shifts to the corresponding 'catch' block where the exception is handled. The catch block essentially serves as our program's safety net, preventing it from crashing due to unhandled exceptions.

Consider a division operation. Here, dividing by zero would throw an ArithmeticException. By placing this operation inside a try-catch block, we can catch this exception and provide a meaningful message to the user instead of allowing the program to crash.

8.3 Finally Block

In addition to try-catch, we also have the 'finally' block. Code within this block will execute whether an exception is thrown or not. It's primarily used for cleanup operations, such as closing database connections or file streams, that need to be performed regardless of whether the operation was successful or not.

8.4 Types of Exceptions

Broadly, exceptions can be classified into two categories: checked and unchecked exceptions. Checked exceptions are those which the compiler expects us to catch, like IOException. On the other hand, unchecked exceptions are derived from RuntimeException and the compiler doesn't mandate to catch them. They usually occur due to programming errors, like NullPointerException or ArrayIndexOutOfBoundsException.

8.5 Custom Exceptions

In addition to the standard exceptions provided by the programming language, we can create our own custom exceptions. Custom exceptions are particularly useful when we want to throw an exception that encapsulates specific business logic or rules.

8.6 Best Practices

A key principle in exception handling is to catch exceptions as late as possible and throw them as early as possible. This ensures that we don't catch an exception before we know how to handle it, and we don't delay throwing it when we detect it.

Also, don't use exceptions for flow control in your programs. Exceptions are meant for exceptional conditions and not to replace conditional (if-else) logic.

When defining custom exceptions, always make them meaningful and specific. A well-named exception can make the debugging process much easier.

Handling exceptions forms a crucial component of the software development process. It equips us with the tools to build robust, error-resistant applications that can handle unexpected situations gracefully. Though we cannot avoid exceptions entirely, we can manage them effectively.

As we wrap up this chapter, remember that exception handling isn't about preventing all errors; it's about anticipating potential problems and knowing how to respond when they occur. Effective exception handling will lead to better user experience, easier maintenance, and overall, more reliable applications. Keep practicing, and soon it'll be second nature for you to write resilient code.

Chapter 9: File Handling: Reading and Writing Data

Navigating the programming seas, we've explored various islands from encapsulation to exception handling. Now, it's time to embark on another crucial voyage - File Handling. Understanding how to interact with files, be it reading or writing data, is an indispensable skill in your coding toolkit. In this chapter, we're going to learn how to sail these waters smoothly.

9.1 Understanding File Handling

At its core, file handling involves creating, reading, writing, and deleting files. It's essentially how your program interacts with files on your system. Whether it's a text file containing user inputs, a CSV file with datasets, or a configuration file with system settings, knowing how to handle these files grants you the ability to tap into a world of data beyond your program's run-time.

9.2 Opening and Closing Files

Before we dive into reading and writing data, it's important to understand how to open and close files. Most languages have built-in functions for this. For example, Python uses the **open()** function to open a file, which returns a file object. This file object is subsequently used for reading, writing, or appending data. Once we're done with the file, it's important to close it using the **close()** method to free up system resources.

9.3 Reading Data from Files

Now that we've seen how to open a file, let's learn to read data from it. Reading files usually involves specifying the mode while opening the file. For instance, in Python, the 'r' mode is used for reading.

Once the file is open in the correct mode, we can read its contents. There are typically methods to read the entire file content at once, or line by line, or even a specific number of characters at a time. How you choose to read largely depends on the file size and your program's specific needs.

9.4 Writing and Appending Data to Files

Writing data to a file is quite similar to reading. Instead of the 'r' mode, we use 'w' for writing. Should the file be non-existent, it will be created. However, if it does exist, the 'w' mode will overwrite the existing file. To add data to an existing file without deleting the current content, we use the 'a' (append) mode.

When writing data, ensure that the data is in the correct format. For instance, if you're writing to a text file, you'll want to ensure the data is converted to a string before writing.

9.5 Dealing with CSV Files

Comma-Separated Values (CSV) files are a common format for storing tabular data, and handling them is a common task in data manipulation. In Python, for instance, the **csv** module provides functionalities to read and write data in CSV format. Other languages provide similar libraries or modules for CSV file handling.

9.6 Error Handling in File Operations

As we learned in the last chapter, things don't always go as planned. The file you're trying to read might not exist, or your program might not have the necessary permissions to write to a file. These situations will raise exceptions. You can and should handle these exceptions to prevent your program from crashing and instead provide useful feedback to the user.

9.7 Working with File Paths

File paths can be absolute or relative. An absolute path begins with the root folder, while a relative path is relative to the program's current working directory. Understanding this difference is crucial when your programs need to work across different operating systems, as different systems have different path syntax.

9.8 Best Practices

Remember to always close files after you're done with them. Leaving files open can consume system resources and may affect the performance of your application. Languages like Python offer a **with** statement, which automatically takes care of closing the file, even if exceptions occur within the block.

Also, avoid reading the entire content of large files at once. Instead, read chunks or lines iteratively, which is more memory-efficient.

File handling is a critical skill set for any programmer. From reading input data to writing logs or results, effective file handling can be the key to developing a robust and efficient application.

As we conclude this chapter, remember, practice is vital. Try out different file operations, handle various data formats, and most importantly, anticipate and deal with potential errors. With time and practice, you'll find file handling as natural as writing a loop or a conditional statement. So, keep coding, keep exploring, and keep learning.

Chapter 10: Introduction to GUI Programming with JavaFX

We've written algorithms, dealt with exceptions, and manipulated files. Now let's venture into a new domain: graphical user interfaces (GUIs). The console is a great tool for interaction, but when it comes to creating user-friendly applications, nothing beats a well-crafted GUI. In this chapter, we'll explore GUI programming using JavaFX, a powerful platform for creating rich internet applications in Java.

10.1 What is JavaFX?

JavaFX is a Java library used to create desktop applications, as well as rich internet applications that can run on various devices. It's a modern replacement for Swing, the older Java GUI toolkit, providing a much cleaner and more intuitive API.

10.2 Setting Up Your Environment

To get started with JavaFX, you need to have a suitable IDE installed, such as IntelliJ IDEA or Eclipse, and the JavaFX SDK. "The SDK can be obtained from the official site for download." Once downloaded, you need to set up the JavaFX library in your IDE. A plethora of online resources and official documentation are available to guide you through the setup process.

10.3 Understanding the JavaFX Architecture

At the heart of every JavaFX application is the Application class. Each JavaFX application needs to extend this class, where you'll define the initial user interface within the **start()** method.

JavaFX applications follow a stage-scene-graph metaphor. The **Stage** class represents the top-level container, or window. Inside this stage, you have a **Scene** that can hold various graphical components. These components are known as nodes, forming a tree-like structure, referred to as a scene graph.

10.4 Layouts and Controls

JavaFX provides a wide range of controls, such as buttons, text fields, checkboxes, and more. These controls can be added to the scene graph to create your user interface.

To organize these controls, JavaFX offers different layouts including **HBox, VBox, GridPane**, and **BorderPane**, among others. Each layout has its own rules for arranging nodes, allowing you to create complex and responsive user interfaces.

10.5 Event Handling

Interactive applications respond to user actions, such as clicks or key presses. In JavaFX, these are handled by registering event handlers on nodes. An event handler is simply a piece of code that's executed in response to a specific event.

For instance, a button click event can be handled by registering an **EventHandler<ActionEvent>** to the button, and providing an **handle()** method that dictates what happens when the button is clicked.

10.6 Styling with CSS

JavaFX adopts web-standard Cascading Style Sheets (CSS) for styling its user interfaces. This allows you to separate the application's look-and-feel from the application logic. JavaFX's CSS is similar to the CSS used in web development, making it a familiar territory for those with web development background.

10.7 Scene Builder

While it's perfectly fine to create your JavaFX UI programmatically, using a tool like Scene Builder can drastically simplify the process. Scene Builder is a visual layout tool that lets you design your JavaFX application interface by dragging and dropping components, and it automatically generates the corresponding FXML code.

As we wrap up this introductory chapter on JavaFX, keep in mind that building an effective GUI is both an art and a science. Understanding the mechanics of JavaFX is crucial, but so is the ability to craft an intuitive, user-friendly interface.

While JavaFX might feel different from what we've covered so far, it's an essential skill for Java programmers. So, dive in, experiment, and start building your own user interfaces. And remember, as with everything else in programming, practice is key.

Chapter 11: Event Handling and User Interaction

With the basics of GUI programming under your belt, it's time to bring your applications to life. A static interface can be attractive, but without the capability to interact with the user, it remains an inert digital painting. In this chapter, we'll unravel the art of event handling and user interaction, adding responsiveness to your applications.

11.1 What is Event Handling?

Event handling in programming refers to how a program responds to actions from the user, system, or another program. These actions, or "events," could be a mouse click, a key press, a system-generated notification, or more.

As a coder, your task is to define "event handlers" - sections of code that respond to specific events. The event triggers the handler, which then executes the code to respond to the event.

11.2 Button Click Event in JavaFX

Let's start with a common event - a button click in JavaFX. You'd start by defining a button:

javaCopy code

Button myButton = new Button("Click me");

Now, let's assign an event handler to this button using a lambda expression:

javaCopy code

myButton.setOnAction(e -> { System.out.println("The button was clicked!"); });

Here, **setOnAction()** is the method we use to register an event handler. The handler itself is a lambda expression, which gets triggered upon the click event. When the button is clicked, "The button was clicked!" will be printed to the console.

11.3 Event Handler for TextField

Now, let's see how we can handle events for a TextField. Let's say we want our program to react when the user presses Enter after typing into a TextField.

javaCopy code

TextField myTextField = new TextField(); myTextField.setOnAction(e -> { System.out.println("You entered: " + myTextField.getText()); });

In this code, **myTextField.getText()** is used to get the text that the user entered. When the user hits Enter, the text field's content will be printed to the console.

11.4 Mouse Events

In addition to keyboard events, GUI applications often respond to mouse events, like clicks, movements, and drags. Let's make our application react to a double-click event.

javaCopy code

```
Scene myScene = new Scene(new Group(), 800, 600);
myScene.setOnMouseClicked(e -> { if (e.getClickCount() == 2) { System.out.println("Double click detected!"); } });
```

Here, we are setting the event handler directly on the scene. The getClickCount() function yields the quantity of mouse clicks tied to the given event. If it's equal to 2, we print a message indicating a double click.

11.5 Understanding Event Types

JavaFX has a wide range of event types that you can handle, from drag-and-drop events to touch events. By handling different event types, you can make your application highly interactive and responsive.

For instance, let's handle a key pressed event. We want to print a message to the console whenever the user presses the spacebar:

javaCopy code

```
myScene.setOnKeyPressed(e  ->  {  if  (e.getCode()  ==
KeyCode.SPACE)      {      System.out.println("Spacebar
pressed!"); } });
```

Here, the **setOnKeyPressed()** method sets the event handler for the key pressed event. The **getCode()** method is used to determine which key was pressed.

11.6 Event Propagation

In JavaFX, events have a specific propagation path. They start at the targeted node and then move up through the parent nodes. This is why an event can be handled by the node that was the target of the event or by any of its parent nodes.

By understanding this event propagation, you can manage and control how events are handled in your application.

Event handling is the heart of interactive programming. It brings your applications to life, allowing users to engage with your software in intuitive and meaningful ways.

As we end this chapter, I encourage you to play around with event handling. Try different event types, play with event propagation, and experiment with various GUI components. Remember, hands-on practice is the best way to cement your understanding and hone your skills. Happy coding!

Chapter 12: Working with Databases: JDBC and SQL

The ability to persist and manipulate data is a cornerstone of modern software applications. Databases are integral to this process, enabling the storage, retrieval, and manipulation of data in an organized manner. This chapter will dive into Java's interaction with databases, using JDBC (Java Database Connectivity) and SQL (Structured Query Language).

12.1 Understanding Databases and SQL

Databases allow you to manage large amounts of data efficiently.

SQL is a standard language used to manage and manipulate relational databases. It provides commands for tasks such as creating tables, inserting records, updating records, and fetching data.

12.2 Introduction to JDBC

JDBC is a Java API that manages connecting to a database, executing commands and queries, and handling result sets obtained from the database. It enables interaction with a wide range of databases, including MySQL, Oracle, and SQLite.

12.3 Setting Up a Database Connection

Before you can interact with a database, you need to establish a connection using the **DriverManager.getConnection()** method. Here's a basic example:

javaCopy code

```
String url = "jdbc:mysql://localhost:3306/myDatabase";
String username = "root"; String password = "root";
Connection connection = DriverManager.getConnection(url, username, password);
```

Remember to close the connection after you're done to free up resources:

javaCopy code

```
connection.close();
```

12.4 Executing SQL Statements

With a connection established, you can execute SQL statements. The **Statement** and **PreparedStatement** interfaces allow you to execute SQL commands.

For example, to execute a SELECT statement:

javaCopy code

```java
String sql = "SELECT * FROM Users"; Statement
statement = connection.createStatement(); ResultSet
resultSet = statement.executeQuery(sql);
```

While executing a query, the returned result is a
ResultSet object, which can be used to iterate over the
resulting records.

12.5 Processing Result Sets

A **ResultSet** provides various methods to process the
returned data. The **next()** method moves the cursor to the
next row, and various getter methods (like **getString()**,
getInt(), etc.) retrieve column values:

12.6 Inserting, Updating, and Deleting Records

Besides querying data, JDBC can execute any SQL
statement.

Similarly, you can update or delete records. Note the use of
executeUpdate(), which returns the number of affected
rows.

12.7 Handling Exceptions

While working with JDBC, various issues can arise, such as
a faulty SQL statement or a lost database connection. These
situations result in exceptions. Using try-catch blocks, you
can handle these exceptions gracefully:

javaCopy code

```
try { // database operations } catch (SQLException e) {
System.out.println("Database operation failed: " +
e.getMessage()); }
```

12.8 Best Practices

While using JDBC, always close your resources (like **Connection**, **Statement**, and **ResultSet**) in a **finally** block or use try-with-resources to automatically close them.

Additionally, consider using **PreparedStatement** over **Statement** to prevent SQL injection attacks and improve performance with batch updates.

By connecting your Java applications to a database using JDBC, you can build robust, data-driven applications. Keep in mind that while this chapter covers the basics, databases encompass a vast domain, and there's much more to explore and learn. Continue honing your skills, and remember that hands-on practice is essential. Happy coding!

Chapter 13: Multithreading: Concurrent Programming in Java

In today's high-demand computing world, executing tasks sequentially or one at a time may not meet modern application needs. Users expect applications to perform tasks concurrently, enhancing efficiency and improving the overall user experience. This chapter introduces multithreading, a key feature in Java that addresses this need by allowing concurrent programming.

13.1 What is a Thread?

In the simplest terms, a thread is a separate path of execution in a program. It's the smallest unit that can be scheduled by an operating system. A single process can contain multiple threads, all running concurrently and potentially performing different tasks.

13.2 Creating a Thread in Java

Java offers two methods for thread creation: one through the extension of the Thread class and another by implementing the Runnable interface.

Extending the Thread class:

javaCopy code

```java
class MyThread extends Thread { public void run() {
System.out.println("Thread is running."); } } public class
Main { public static void main(String[] args) { MyThread
myThread = new MyThread(); myThread.start(); } }
```

Implementing the Runnable interface:

javaCopy code

```java
class MyRunnable implements Runnable { public void
run() { System.out.println("Thread is running."); } } public
class Main { public static void main(String[] args) { Thread
myThread = new Thread(new MyRunnable());
myThread.start(); } }
```

In both cases, the **run()** method contains the code to be
executed in the thread. **start()** method is called to initiate
the thread's execution.

13.3 Thread States and Life Cycle

- *New:* A newly created thread that has not yet
  started.

- *Runnable:* A thread that is executing in the JVM.

Understanding these states is crucial for managing thread
execution effectively.

13.4 Thread Synchronization

When multiple threads access shared resources, conflicts can arise. Synchronization is a mechanism that regulates the access of multiple threads to shared resources. In Java, we use the **synchronized** keyword to achieve this:

javaCopy code

```
class Counter { int count; synchronized void increment() {
count++; } } public class Main { public static void
main(String[] args) { Counter c = new Counter(); Thread t1
= new Thread(() -> { for (int i = 0; i < 1000; i++) {
c.increment(); } }); Thread t2 = new Thread(() -> { for (int i
= 0; i < 1000; i++) { c.increment(); } }); t1.start();
t2.start(); // join the threads to ensure count is updated
after both threads finish t1.join(); t2.join();
System.out.println("Count: " + c.count); } }
```

Here, only one thread can access the **increment()** method at a time, preventing any interference between them.

13.5 Thread Communication

Threads can communicate with each other using **wait()**, **notify()**, and **notifyAll()** methods. These methods are used in synchronized context to allow threads to wait for resources to become available and to notify other threads when resources have become available.

13.6 Thread Pool

Creating a new thread for every task can be expensive in terms of time and resources. A thread pool is a group of pre-instantiated threads ready to execute tasks.

Multithreading is a powerful concept that allows for concurrent programming in Java. While we've touched on many of the key aspects of multithreading in this chapter, mastering multithreading requires time, practice, and a deep understanding of the principles behind concurrent computing.

From creating and managing threads, to understanding their lifecycle, synchronizing their tasks, and even pooling them for efficient resource management, we've covered a lot of ground. Take your time to digest these concepts, practice with hands-on examples, and explore the rich API that Java provides for multithreaded programming. Remember, the journey of learning is gradual, and each step forward brings you closer to mastering the art of multithreaded programming. Happy coding!

Chapter 14: Advanced Topics: Generics, Lambda Expressions, and Streams

As we venture deeper into Java, it becomes imperative to acquaint ourselves with some advanced topics that can significantly enhance your coding skills and broaden your understanding of the language. In this chapter, we'll explore Generics, Lambda Expressions, and Streams, all of which play a vital role in developing robust and efficient Java applications.

14.1 Generics

Generics add stability to your code by allowing you to specify, at compile time, the specific types that a collection can contain, or a method can operate upon. This feature helps prevent runtime type-casting errors and adds a layer of abstraction.

For example, here's a generic method that accepts an object of any type and prints it:

```java
javaCopy code
public static    void print
```

And here's how you might use generics with collections:

javaCopy code

```
                    new ArrayList                "Alice"
        "Bob"
```

14.2 Lambda Expressions

Lambda expressions are a fundamental part of Java's shift towards functional programming. They provide a concise way to represent one method interface using an expression. Lambda expressions are beneficial for event handling and data processing.

javaCopy code

5

14.3 Streams

Streams in Java 8 are a major abstraction that simplify operations on sets of data. Streams are particularly useful when working with large amounts of data, as they can optimize and simplify tasks such as filtering, mapping, or iterating over collections.

Here's an example of using a Stream to filter and print elements:

```
javaCopy code
                              "Alice"  "Bob"  "Charlie"
"David"                                        "A"
```

14.4 Digging Deeper into Generics

Generics are more than just parameterized types for
collections. They can also be used in class, interface, and
method declarations.

A simple generic class could look like this:

14.5 Lambda Expressions and Functional Interfaces

Lambda expressions are typically used to implement
methods defined by functional interfaces - interfaces that
declare a single abstract method. Java 8 offers numerous
pre-defined functional interfaces contained within the
java.util.function package.

For instance, the **Predicate** interface represents a simple
condition or boolean-valued function:

```
javaCopy code
```

14.6 Advanced Stream Operations

Streams provide a rich API for manipulating data. You can chain multiple operations together in a pipeline, which can be parallelized for efficiency.

Here are some advanced Stream operations:

Mapping:

javaCopy code

```
1  2  3  4  5
```

Reducing:

javaCopy code

```
1  2  3  4  5   int sum

0
```

Generics, Lambda expressions, and Streams are advanced concepts that can help you write more flexible, efficient, and robust code. Understanding and effectively using these features will significantly enhance your Java programming skills.

As with any new concept, it takes practice to become comfortable using these tools. Experiment with Generics to make your code more flexible and safer. Use Lambda expressions to make your code more concise and readable. Take advantage of Streams to efficiently manipulate data.

Keep pushing your boundaries, continue practicing, and keep exploring the fascinating world of Java programming. Happy coding!

Chapter 15: Unit Testing and Debugging: Ensuring Code Reliability

Developing an application is not just about writing code that works. It's about creating reliable, maintainable code that behaves as expected under a range of conditions. In this chapter, we're going to explore two crucial aspects of ensuring code reliability - unit testing and debugging.

15.1 The Importance of Testing

Testing plays a pivotal role in software development. It verifies that your code functions as expected and helps identify any bugs or issues that could impact the software's performance or reliability. A comprehensive set of tests can give you the confidence that your code is ready for deployment and that future changes won't unexpectedly break existing functionality.

15.2 Unit Testing with JUnit

In Java, JUnit is one of the most commonly used frameworks for unit testing. A unit test verifies the functionality of a small part of the code, such as a single method or class. JUnit provides annotations to specify test methods and assertions to check the expected results.

Here's a simple example:

javaCopy code

```
import org.junit.Test; import static
org.junit.Assert.assertEquals; public class CalculatorTest {
@Test public void testAddition() { Calculator calculator =
new Calculator(); int result = calculator.add(2, 3);
assertEquals(5, result); } }
```

In this example, we're testing the **add** method of a
Calculator class. The **assertEquals** method is used to
check if the result of the method matches the expected
output.

15.3 Debugging

Even with thorough testing, bugs can still make their way
into your code. Debugging involves the procedure of
identifying and rectifying these problems. This can involve
reading code, using a debugging tool to step through code
and inspect values, or adding print statements to output
values at certain points.

Java IDEs like IntelliJ IDEA and Eclipse come with
powerful debuggers that allow you to set breakpoints, step
through code, inspect variables, and more.

15.4 Writing Effective Unit Tests

Writing unit tests is a skill that takes practice to develop. Here are some tips to help you write effective unit tests:

1. **Make each test independent:** Tests should not rely on other tests or on the state of external systems.

2. **Test one thing at a time:** Each test should verify one piece of functionality.

3. **Use meaningful names:** The name of a test should clearly state what functionality it's testing.

4. **Check for both success and failure:** Don't just test the "happy path." Also test how your code behaves when something goes wrong.

15.5 Advanced Debugging Techniques

Advanced debugging involves more than setting breakpoints and stepping through code. Here are a few techniques that can help you debug more effectively:

1. **Exception Breakpoints:** This allows the program to pause whenever a specific exception occurs.

2. **Conditional Breakpoints:** This allows the program to pause only when a particular condition is met.

3. **Logging:** This involves writing information about the program's execution to a log file to be analyzed later.

15.6 Automating Testing with Continuous Integration

Continuous Integration (CI) is a practice where developers integrate their code into a shared repository frequently, often several times a day. Each integration is then automatically built and tested, allowing teams to detect problems early. Tools like Jenkins, Travis CI, and GitHub Actions can automate the build and test process.

The processes of unit testing and debugging are indispensable elements in software creation, assuring the trustworthiness of your programming code. Learning to write effective tests and use debugging tools will not only make your applications more robust but also make you a better developer.

Remember, a successful programmer isn't just someone who can write code, but someone who can write code that stands the test of time. As you progress on your programming journey, keep the concepts of testing and debugging close to heart and let them guide you towards writing impeccable, reliable code.

The road to mastery may seem long and arduous, but remember that every line of code you write, every bug you fix, and every test you pass brings you one step closer to your goal. Keep striving, keep learning, and never stop pushing the boundaries of what you can achieve. Happy coding!

Conclusion

As we conclude this comprehensive exploration of Java programming, it's important to remember that our journey in learning never truly ends. The field of computer science and programming is dynamic, continually evolving and presenting new challenges and opportunities. What you've learned in this book is a strong foundation, a springboard from which you can dive deeper into the vast ocean of knowledge that is programming.

Throughout this book, we've ventured through the basic constructs of the Java language, understanding variables, data types, operators, and control flow structures. We've explored the principles of object-oriented programming, delving into concepts such as classes, objects, inheritance, polymorphism, and interfaces.

We went further into arrays, collections, and data structures, learning how to efficiently store and manipulate data. We took an in-depth look at exception handling and the importance of writing robust code that can deal with unexpected scenarios gracefully.

We've examined the importance of File I/O, understanding how our applications can interact with external data. We then moved on to creating graphical user interfaces with

JavaFX, learned about event handling, and discovered how to create interactive applications.

We've delved into database interactions with JDBC and SQL, learning to build applications that can persist and retrieve data from databases. We also discovered the world of concurrent programming with multithreading and explored advanced topics like generics, lambda expressions, and streams.

Finally, we underscored the importance of code reliability with unit testing and debugging, highlighting practices that can help us write better, more resilient code.

Remember, though, that understanding these concepts is only the first step. Practice is key in programming. Write code every day. Challenge yourself with new problems. Collaborate with others, contribute to open-source projects, or develop your own. The more you code, the more you will learn, and the better you will get.

In this dynamic field, learning is an ongoing process. Stay curious, stay updated. Read articles, join forums, attend webinars and workshops. Never lose the zeal to learn and improve.

As you continue your journey, remember that programming is not just about writing code or building applications. It's about problem-solving, it's about creativity, and most importantly, it's about continuous learning.

Thank you for being a part of this journey. It's been a pleasure to guide you through the world of Java programming, and we hope you feel better equipped and inspired to continue exploring and learning.

Best of luck on your coding journey. Happy coding!

References

1. Bloch, J. (2018). *Effective Java (3rd ed.).* Addison-Wesley Professional.

2. Deitel, P. J., & Deitel, H. M. (2018). *Java: How to Program, Early Objects (11th ed.).* Pearson.

3. Eckel, B. (2006). *Thinking in Java (4th ed.).* Prentice Hall.

4. Sierra, K., & Bates, B. (2005). *Head First Java (2nd ed.).* O'Reilly Media.

5. JUnit Team (2021). *JUnit 5 User Guide.* [Online] Available:

   https://junit.org/junit5/docs/current/user-guide/

6. Oracle Corporation (2021). *Java Platform, Standard Edition (Java SE) 11.* Oracle Help Center. [Online] Available:

   https://docs.oracle.com/en/java/javase/11/

7. Oracle Corporation (2021). *JavaFX Documentation Project.* Oracle. [Online] Available:

   https://openjfx.io/javadoc/11/

Please note that the field of computer science and programming is constantly evolving. The cited resources are accurate as of the time of publication, but it's always good practice to look for the most recent and up-to-date resources.

www.ingramcontent.com/pod-product-compliance
Lightning Source LLC
LaVergne TN
LVHW051746050326
832903LV00029B/2756